MEN SHOULD COME WITH WARNING LABELS

Sonia Torretto

Men Should Come With Warning Labels

Originally published in The United States by RFP

PRINTING HISTORY

RFP first edition published November 2006

ISBN-10: 0-6151-3664-8

ISNN-13: 978-0-6151-3664-6

Set in 11/12pt Century School Book by KBR Inc. Atlanta GA, USA

Reproduced and bound in The United States by Lulu Publishing
www.lulu.com

This book is dedicated to all the women who read it.

And to all the men who gave me the material.

THE MEN

INTRODUCTION

T his book is a little correspondence about, well, some tidbits that I have learned about men. I am a 41-year-old professional woman, who has been married, divorced, single, married again, and divorced again. I am presently single. To add interest to the situation, I am a therapist, and I specialize with teenagers. In my practice I have observed that many grown men share many characteristics with teenagers, so I have a lot of information, from a lot of sources. Of course, at 41, I have more experience than I care to admit. But, I figure, why not put this information to good use? Maybe others can learn from my experiences. I must admit that I have been a slow learner when it comes to affairs of the heart. I hope that by writing about what I have observed you, the reader, can benefit from my experience and help you, *and me*, avoid some of these heartaches

This book is designed to be simple, direct and hopefully humorous.

I have written from my own experiences, and those of some close friends (with their permission), because I wanted the book to be real and relevant. We are all human, and we all make mistakes. I still make them, not as many, and not for as long, but I still make them and they still hurt. So, some of the accounts are personal. They may appear to be too personal, but I hope that you will see the truth in them and the humor. It won't be hard, I assure you.

I always say that men are interesting creatures. But I know that this is an over generalization. Not all men are interesting, and not all men are creatures. I am still looking for that healthy balance of a man. He's out there somewhere, or at least my mom and all my attached friends keep telling me so. We will see. I think it's about setting better boundaries and being more honest and realistic with ourselves. I am not looking for the "perfect relationship". I don't even know if I want a relationship sometimes. But, I do know that I still love men and I still crave to understand and grow in my relationships with them and ultimately, with myself. It's progress, not perfection. Thank goodness, otherwise, as a therapist, I'd be out of a job.

I used to spend a lot of time (too much time) trying to figure out why I can't or haven't found that one special person. I listened to other people who would say that I was too picky or too intimidating, and that you can't have it all. Men are either smart or attractive, and you can't have both. But I want both. So that led me to the thought that, if they can't be both, I can't be both. I always felt that I was not perfect enough, and it's very easy to reinforce that fear based thought. Nobody is perfect and striving for that perfection reinforces your own inadequacies. You've probably done it too, focused on the crazy thoughts that everyone was prettier or skinnier or basically more marketable than yourself. I figured I was smart, and I have the rap sheet to prove it, so that ruled out being pretty. So, dating good-looking guys was a type of validation for me. If they liked me, that meant that I was attractive, but it also meant that I might not be smart. See the dilemma?

Being intelligent and resourceful was very important and necessary when I was growing up, because I wanted to learn how to make a living for myself. I am the product of an immigrant family system. Both sides of my family came into the United States through Ellis Island in the early 1900's...before women could vote. Some say that it takes three generations to Americanize, so I am about there. But there is still that drive that I needed to be self sufficient and independent. That's what I was taught, and my dad said that I would never have to depend on a man. Guess I took that pretty literally. It's a juvenile thought process, I know, until it's yours! Then it seems very literal and can hold a lot of strength in the way you build your relationships and attach value to them. I always find it interesting how we can take the right concept and attach it to the wrong relationship or visa versa. Anyway, it all comes down to this: You can't find your true partner if you are not true to yourself. That's the bottom line.

And just so you know, nowadays, I like attractive men because I am attracted to them. There's no weird agenda, and I don't care what other people say. I date who I want to date, based on what I want. In the end my reflections, my learning experiences, and my issues, are my concern. We shouldn't judge other people. We could, instead, choose to be realistic about what the issues are, and how that applies to us. Expectations are just setups for resentments anyway, and what's the point in that?

Did you ever think about how women got into the situation that we are in? I mean, really. Is it rocket science or what? What happened to the clear set of rules? The rule being the concept of the man courting the woman and the woman setting the boundaries. I think it was too extreme in the 40's and 50's, but I think the *idea* was pretty on target. The roles were clear and defined. Granted they needed to be redefined with the whole, "woman's place is in the home" thing, but there was clarity in how to date and treat each other. Or at least that's the way it seems to me. The 60's, of course, was the time of redefinition. The 70's was the attempt at balance and the 80's was the "forget it, I'll just do it all myself" era. So, what are we left with? More redefining. Men are confused, women are confused, children are confused. Who is at home? Who works? Who is divorced? Who the hell is not divorced? Who's on first?? Where's the balance? The synchronicity? How do we know what the right thing is? Well, I am going to give you my take on it.

The last thing that I have to say before we get on with things is that it's important to recognize the unhealthy things that can't change. I do this much, much quicker these days. In other words, I pay attention to the reality of the situation, not the fantasy in my mind, as Melodie Beattie says. I also try to remember that the value in love is through giving without expectation, so be careful who you give to, so as not to sabotage that value. That just came out of my head, isn't that good?

Here's what I think that I know:

All behavior has a purpose: attention, power, revenge or inadequacy. This statement is from Adlerian theory, which also focuses a lot on belonging. That's a therapy thing.

We act out what we learn in our family system and we recreate our family system wherever we go. Think about it. It's really true.

Men will do the weirdest things to connect with you and then the weirdest things to disconnect.

It takes about a month to know a man. I'll let you think about that one.

When a man wants to be with a woman, wild horses can't keep him away. Men will go to great lengths to be with the woman that they want. It doesn't matter if it is a challenge. They will do what is necessary, especially if they know it's important or it will impress you. It's what happens after they get you that is your responsibility.

There is love and there is fear, and they both can't exist simultaneously. This is from <u>A Course In Miracles</u>. My interpretation is that you cannot be in "fear based thought" and "unconditional loving thought" at the same time. You have to choose. If you stay in your fear, you will get more of the same. If you stay in unconditional acceptance with yourself and others, you will get that back as well.

The ego is fear.

Unconditional love is the most important thing.

We are all soul-mates. We can all be friends... if our souls touch, we are a soul-mate of sorts.

Relationships are reflections. You will get sick of reading this. We learn through relationship. That's why we act out what we learn in our families, or lack there of. It's the first relationship that we really have to extract value and reflect from. Life is like a bunch of mirrors... I guess that's why it's so confusing sometimes. There can be too many reflections at the same time and you have to figure out which is causing what.

We seek out in others what we see in ourselves. It's the law of attraction. And it's similar to the reflection thing. Think about it.

We are all one consciousness.

Focus your energies on what you want. Don't waste any time on what you don't want.

Great sex has an expiration date.

So... let the fun begin.

Your man should come with a warning label if he is...

...the HAS ISSUES WITH HIS MOM MAN

Well, this is a biggie and encompasses so, so many other concepts, so take it slow. We have the:

A. My mom is an alcoholic.

B. My mom cheated on my dad.

C. My mom is a lesbian.

D. My mom is a nut.

E. My mom treated me like an object.

F. My mom is evil.

G. My mom is God.

No matter what the issue, and I have heard them all, we can diagnose it, pick it apart, make excuses for it, hope, pray, scream or holler... the end result is still the same. He needs a big warning label and lots of therapy. Unless he develops a pretty keen awareness, which is possible, but not likely, forget it. He will be the one who seeks revenge on every woman he is with. He will avoid attachment, avoid commitment, be too busy, and ultimately be emotionally unavailable. The unfortunate thing... he will probably be pretty and he will come across really thoughtful and kind at first. But just give him a month, and he will show his true colors. His biggest fear is abandonment, and his goal is to get back at his mom. Keep in mind that she is who taught him how to treat women. Think about where that leaves you. It's "left" me lots of times.

...the I HATE MY DAD MAN.

So... this is the man he modeled after. Great. Two choices... one is he becomes the opposite of whom he thought his dad was or two he recreates it. It's two that we are worried about. Keep in mind the "we act out what we learn in our family and recreate it wherever we go" concept. Whether his dad was an alcoholic, evil, abusive, a cheater, gay, etc., it's about responsibility and the lengths he will go, to overcome and break patterns of behavior.

Blah, Blah, La La... it takes a long time. How long are you willing to wait? How committed is he to working on it? How mean is he? That, by the way, is never ok.

I don't know about you, but this is not what I call relationship material.

Don't stay with the man you don't want just because he is the man you are with at the time.

...the INVADING YOUR PERSONAL SPACE MAN

He could also be called the "up your butt" man. He can't know enough about you. He calls 15 times a day and wants to talk for hours. You wonder if he has a job, a life, a thought process, a dog... make it stop, I am exhausted! What's your favorite color, flower, dog, cat, restaurant, beer, wine, store, mall, car, city, state, country. Stop it please! He can't wait to fall in love with you, but really he just hates being alone. This guy turns into the control freak later. Then you feel cheated, because it was never really about you. It's about him and he is...

Over-protective

Over-the edge

OVER-THE TOP!

...the ONLY CHILD MAN

C an you say self centered? Egocentric? These people have to learn to share already. Enough said. They need too much alone time.

p.s. The ones that learn to share well are actually pretty cool!

...the **RESCUER MAN**

This is the guy who creates crap to rescue you from. If he can't find anything, he gets critical with you and picks apart your life. No thanks. I am already hard enough on myself. I don't need to reinforce that which I create on my own!! Just cut my grass. Rescue me from that.

...the ACTIVELY USING DRUGS MAN

R un !!!   Away as fast as you can. Buy <u>Codependent No More</u>, and read it three times. Do not pass go, do not collect 200 dollars. Don't try to fix it, understand it, help it, support it, etc. Just run. It is much, much bigger than you.

I married this. It wasn't pretty... ever... and it didn't have a good ending.

But seriously, if you are just dating this guy, get out before you marry him. Go to al-anon, and to therapy, and start to figure out why you feel that you need to take care of someone who is on such a path. This issue is so big, and so involved that I could write a book on it, just based on my experience. I just might one day.

Addiction encompasses every aspect of life, all at once. So, if you want your mental, emotional, and physical existence to be turned upside down and sideways, and shaken up in a blender on the chop setting... stay. But remember, you didn't cause it, can't control it, and won't cure it (that's from al-anon). And no matter what he says, you are not powerful enough for it to be your fault. Your job is to look at how you participate and focus on what you can change to make your life better.

Your mantra to him should be, "I trust you will work it out" (but probably not with me).

But getting as far away as possible is the best solution.

...the STEROID MAN

Why? Why is this necessary? Why would anyone want to look like the Pillsbury doughboy? Who finds that attractive? I don't. Then there are the bad temper, personality changes, chemical dependence and medical problems that go with it. Fun. What a great foundation for a mutually respectful relationship.

...the SPORTS NUT MAN

This is the guy who is obsessed with every sport known to mankind. His life is planned around what game is on and who is going to watch it with him. Makes you want to program every TV and radio with the ballet.

Boring!

...the NOT CUTE, BUT THINKS HE IS MAN

T his is funny. What is it about guys and their looks? Why do they think that they can have a woman who works out every day and dresses well and has a good 'hair guy', when they haven't worked out in years, go to great clips, and eat mashed potatoes on a daily basis? What is that? Sucking in your gut is not a substitute for a six-pack.

The really good-looking guys know they are hot and want every girl to tell them so. The average guys want a trophy. Well, at least the regular guys can pick one and stick with it. Never mind, I know that's not always true. But... No matter what, they are always looking over their shoulder, just in case. Insecurity comes in many packages. I rode a ski lift with a guy once who told me that if he were married to Claudia Schiffer, he would still be looking over his shoulder for the "better one". He said that men were pigs.

Ok then...

...the JUST TOO BUSY MAN

Too busy for what? You? A bath? A job? A life? No... a girlfriend. He is too busy for a girlfriend because he wants more than one. He is too insecure to open his heart and get to know you. Why? Well, he probably has issues with his mom. (I am sort of kidding) If he gets to know you, he might get a little attached. Oh no! He might want to talk to you more, or ask your advice... yikes! Then he is closed off to every other woman. He might miss out on one.

Too bad.

Well, you aren't missing much. These guys usually aren't very good in bed because they never land long enough to learn how to please a woman. Oh, wait a minute, there's a woman? Right, it's just about him.

This is similar to several other warning label guys, like the "I don't date guy" and the "mixed message man" and the "can't decide guy" and the, well... lots of them.

I say, learn to multi task already... it's part of being a grownup.

...the I'LL CALL YOU IN A FEW DAYS MAN

Yeah... sure you will. Take care. That's what they say when they hang up... "Take care". The key here is to not give him your number in the first place...

...the I DON'T DATE MAN

O h please!!!! Are you gay? Or just an asshole? *"I don't date because I don't have time."* A guy just recently said that to me. I rationalized it because he was young. I asked, *"What are we doing?"* He said that we were dating, but only because we had already *"done stuff"*, whatever that means. He really wanted to slow down because he was feeling obligated, and it was interrupting his schedule. His schedule!!!! I was interrupting his schedule. No kidding... I was behind fishing, hanging out with his friends, work and his workouts. But really, there is no excuse. When a man wants to be with you, he does what is necessary. If he is nice, he does more than is necessary because he wants to impress you. Not having time for me does not impress me. This is the same guy who told me he read a book on how to be a gentleman. I have to find that damn book.

Too bad... he was really hot, but had issues with his mom.

Surprise!

...the NEVER CALLS AGAIN MAN

Ok... this one, I am over. Tell me the chapter in the *"How to be a gentleman"* book where it says that it is acceptable to date a woman, make plans, tell her how beautiful she is, talk about the future, sleep with her, cook her dinner, sleep with her more (even though he needs major improvement), spend the night, call every day... sometimes more than once, etc. etc. and then... then... never call again. What the hell is that? I really want to know. Is this some new form of being passive? Well, it's not new, I know. I just do not get it. I could understand if it's someone you just met and went out with a couple of times, but geeeeeze!

The bad thing is that these guys give us lots of red flags, usually. Do we follow them? No. Why? Because we think it will change and we hope that we are the ones to help it to change. (Because they told us how special we were) Guess what? These guys have issues with their moms (kidding, but not really). I know I always say that. Unfortunately, it's usually true. These guys are cowards.

Guys... quit doing this. Just call when you know we won't answer and say "I don't want to do this" or "I can't" or "I plan on going into a coma on Monday"... just say something.

And... guys... just so you all know, spending time with you does not mean that we want to marry you.

...the **PRETEND MAN**

This is the man who seems to have all these things in common with you. He loves to antique shop (sure he does), loves to go to the mall. Shoes... they are his thing. He cooks, cleans, loves cats, will cut your grass (that will keep coming up), always hangs up the wet towel, and... doesn't care how long it takes for you to have an orgasm, so have as many as you can, because you have about a month. That's all it takes. That's all I have to say.

P.S. You shouldn't be sleeping with a guy that soon. The orgasm thing is a joke ... well, sort of.

...the IT'S BEEN 3 DATES, LET'S DO IT MAN

This is the guy who takes you to approximately one nice restaurant, one pub and cooks for you.

Then, for the next "gathering" he changes it up and says, *"I want to have sex"*.

I really, really had a guy do this.

He just said, *"I don't want to go out on our date, I want to have sex."*

To top it off, he was really surprised when I said, "Are you nuts?"

He had absolutely no excuse.

He was old enough to know better, had been married and was educated.

I suppose he thought he had done "due diligence" in the relationship thus far and figured it was time for me to pay up.

Instead he went bankrupt.

See...

...took about a month.

...the "YOU ARE CUTE AND ALL, BUT YOU AIN'T MODEL MATERIAL MAN"

Yup... happened. We go out for pizza and he sees the so-called *"girl of his dreams"* and can't stop looking at her. He says to me... *"You are cute and all Sonia, but she's model material... I could see her face on the cover of a magazine."* No kidding. Then, of course, he tries to put his tongue in my mouth and says *"Don't worry, I still think you are hot... it's just that I could never have a woman like that."*

Oh... I'm not worried.

Interesting, really, how insecurity comes in so many packages. I guess it's easier to make me feel insecure (you know, so I'll want him more???), than to just take responsibility and be accountable for his own issues.

In reality, he wasn't too sure if he could have *me*. Bringing me down might increase his chances a little... because I would see how cool he really is. Yeah, ok.... sure. Keep me desperate.

In actuality, I liked to hang out with this guy because we had some similar spiritual views and it was fun and interesting to discuss them. His actions were an interesting take on unconditional-ness and respect.

Anyway, this man actually had the initiative to come clean...and apologize. He even said that he was just being insecure. So there is hope! He has been a supportive and generous friend ever since.

...The EXTREMELY CUTE MAN

T his guy comes with a vast number of issues... and here are a few:

He may like to talk to lots of girls so that he can get his "we think you are so hot" fix.

He may worry that you are as cute as he is.

He may get very critical about you and how you look and what you wear and how you do your makeup and hair.

He may be gay.

He may be selfish in and out of bed.

He may think he's missing out on something or someone else.

I am a total sucker for pretty boys. Some of the best relationships that I have had have been with men that I have thought were really attractive. There is nothing wrong with that. But, sometimes, they have those narcissistic, insecure issues. This doesn't surprise me, because I am insecure about my looks and I know that I seek out in others, what I see in myself. Try to watch out for those flags. But don't think that I don't know how hard it is to pay attention when the guy is really, really hot. As hot as you think he is, he can still be a balanced, considerate individual.

You know what else? I have found that these guys are really lazy in bed. Know why? Well, what woman wants to chance losing the hot guy by telling him that he doesn't cut it in the bedroom? It's easier to just fake it and hope that maybe it will improve the next time. So the guy thinks a woman can have an orgasm in 20 seconds or just by the mere sight of him. Hey, it's working for him... why change it. That my friends, is a deal breaker for me.

...the SMALL PENIS MAN

Ok, ok... I know we all hate to talk about this, but it is reality. There are certain things about size that matter. Here is my opinion. I think that if a guy is not 'as well endowed as others', he can make up for it in other ways. We all know what those ways are... I do not have to go into it. But for God sakes... do it. Don't think that we aren't going to notice. There are lots of ways to 'rock my world'. **Go there**. And... a woman's sexuality is not just physical. Cutting my grass 'rocks my world' too. So does picking me up from the airport, and sending flowers, and taking my dog for a walk, and fixing me dinner, and emptying my dishwasher, and washing my car and working out with me and of course talking and snuggling... all good forms of foreplay. It's a mind/body experience.

...the BIG PENIS MAN

This guy wants everyone to see his penis... and, rightfully so, probably. But just because he has that, doesn't mean he doesn't have to do some of the things on the previous page. He just doesn't have to do as many... I am kidding. It's still a mind/body experience.

...the NO WEEKEND MAN

I t's just so fun to date this guy. You work all week and look forward to a nice dinner and a movie, or a picnic and a hike... but he has plans with the guys. Yes, all weekend. After all, he only has a couple of days off and he should be able to choose what he wants to do. But, oddly enough, it just so happens, that on Monday... he is really horny. It's because, "I've been thinking about you all weekend, baby, and besides, absence makes the heart grow fonder. I'm with you almost all week!" Yeah, you're here all week because you like home cooked food and your clothes washed. Besides, my sheets are clean and my shampoo smells better. Not to mention, there is food in the fridge, and there are clean dishes in the cabinet.

Well, that whole 'absence makes the heart grow fonder' thing just pisses me off, to be honest. It's an excuse to not be accountable. Who wants that? But, we allow it and that's why men still do it. We say to ourselves that something is better than nothing.

I would rather have nothing... because it really is something... something more than that anyway.

He's also known as the "play house" guy. Sounds like being married with no fringe benefits. Although... everyone always talks about all these fringe benefits, but what are they, really?

...the MARRIED MAN

O k... do I even need to discuss this?

What are you doing?

It's time to look at your concept of emotional availability... Not in him, but in yourself.

So you think he won't do it to you too????

It's senseless and selfish. There is no way to have a happy ending and nine times out of ten, it won't be in your favor anyway. Just don't do it. This decision affects too many people and some of them may be children. Moreover, it's not your job to fill in his emotional gaps, or be his sounding board and sexual release, regardless of how sad his story seems to be.

Besides, you shouldn't be doing my job for free.

...the MONOGAMOUSLY CHALLENGED MAN

There are two types of monogamously challenged men... the honest, and the not so honest. Not that either one is any more acceptable, but... what are you gonna do... it is what it is.

So, you have the guy with the girlfriend or 'live in' who likes to get some on the side. Sometimes, he will be straight and say, "Hey look, I want to get some on the side... you up for it?" Other times he will just say that he is attached, but not married. In other words, they 'date' other people or have an open relationship. These guys lead you to believe that they will date you, you know, out in public, and that there is a possibility, that maybe, just maybe, he will like you better. But, they don't usually date you in public and they don't want to invest anything. It's just a game (for their ego and at your expense), and its just sex. Doesn't mean they don't like you or anything... it just doesn't mean anything.

The other monogamously challenged man just doesn't tell you that he is challenged at all. You are the challenge. He does what he needs to do or say to get you, and, whomever else he is challenged by, and when you find out... you just don't hear from him again or he says... "Well, it's not like we are serious. It's just fun, right??? I never said I wanted to be serious or in a r-e-l-a-t-i-o-n-s-h-i-p". Yeah, right. Thanks.

I think that the key here is to investigate. If you can't get straight answers, walk away, and try not to sleep with him. Just, walk away, before you get attached. He's not looking out for your best interests. Remember, pay attention to the reality of the situation, not the fantasy in your mind. Unless, of course, he cuts your grass.

...the WHY CAN'T YOU BE PERFECT MAN

Of course, he is perfect. His mom told him so, and I guess it made sense to him at the time. This is the guy who really does think he is the greatest thing since peanut butter. Therefore, he deserves the ultimate woman and everything that 'he' feels goes along with that. Bad hair days, sweat pants with a T-shirt days, no makeup days, have the flu days and don't feel like making him the center of the universe days... not allowed. Not in the plan, and if you can't follow the rules, you're out of there. Remember, you are there for him, so if he needs his house cleaned or his back rubbed, be at attention.

And, you guessed it... issues with mom. Predominate theme, isn't it. Can you say narcissist?

How about this? "I'm sorry Sonia, you just aren't pretty enough, and I don't like the shape of your butt. I've told you a million times, and you just won't work on it. I know that you don't have time to work out for four hours a day and that you have a career, but I want what I want, and I should have that if it's important to me."

All right then... how about looking in the mirror ... start there. Focusing on his own personal growth was obviously, not his forte. Unfortunately, that little scenario happened too. Yeah, I've had a string of them, haven't I. Must be stamped on my forehead. I know, I know... issues with my mom, right?

...the **BAD BOY MAN**

T hese guys can be so attractive, can't they? The total alter ego. They stay out late, take risks, play in a band, have motorcycles, let their hair grow, they are spontaneous and just dance to the beat of their own drums.

How fun is that?

Well, it's great fun for a while. Then a steady job and just a little dependability sounds real fun. So do nice dinners and relaxing in front of the fireplace... and a trip to Aspen sounds nice too.

There's a lot to be said for stability and a vehicle with windows.

...the DOESN'T ORDER YOUR FOOD FOR YOU MAN

I saw this happen the other day and I could not believe it.

I walked into this little deli and there was a woman, in line, in front of me. Her boyfriend or guy friend or brother, for all I know, came in and stood with her for a minute. She said that she was going to go outside and grab a table that had just opened up (it was crowded) and he stayed in line. He spent some of his 'line time' flirting with me. Do you know that when it was his turn, he ordered his food and didn't order her anything?! He didn't even order her a drink. She got irritated with him and he told her that there was no reason for her to be angry. Her food was her responsibility. He sat down at the table that she had saved, and ate his lunch. After all, he didn't know what she wanted to order, and I guess he just doesn't have good command of the English language and couldn't frickin ASK!

What really bothered me was that she stayed at the table. I couldn't be responsible for my actions at that point. Maybe she hasn't known him a month yet.

His other name is "SELFISH MAN"...

Weirdo!

...the METROSEXUAL MAN

This is the guy that you say... *"Wait a minute, are you sure you're a guy?"* This one is hard to distinguish for me... could be the "PRETEND MAN", could be the "COME ON STRONG MAN", could be "just plain old gay".

They don't like sports and don't watch them. They like antiques, and shopping and they are always concerned about their hair and their clothes and their tan. When a guy is that concerned about his shoes, it's time to ask some questions. The other red flag is a low sex drive. So, I don't have the right equipment, or what? When they say, "I go for years without sex and I don't really care if we have sex or not", it's time to rethink the relationship.

Who knows... maybe he is just in touch with his feminine side. I have a friend whom I call a 'girl with a penis'. But when you really get to know him... he's a guy.

Takes about a month, I guess! If he turns out to be gay, he can be the gay guy you saw naked... like in *"Will and Grace"*.

...the COMMITMENT PHOBIC MAN

There isn't one woman out there who hasn't experienced this because it starts in middle school. I could write a book on this topic and of course, many have.

He is the "MIXED MESSAGE MAN", "RATIONALIZER MAN", "MONOGAMOUSLY CHALLENGED MAN", the "JUST TOO BUSY MAN", "NEVER CALLS AGAIN MAN", "I DON'T DATE MAN", "COME ON STRONG MAN", "BOOTIE CALL MAN" etc. etc. etc.

He is all of these all over again.

So why mention it?

I don't know... it just needs to be said again, I guess.

Also, it's probably good to remind all of you that you can't change the outcome of the situation, and that it doesn't pay to find ways to be hopeful, that his 'time has come'. You know what I mean... the 'maybe he's ready' routine.

When a guy is ready to settle, that is exactly what he does. He looks around and says... I think I'll get married now. Maybe he's run out of things to do. Maybe he's tired. Maybe he's ready for another income. Who knows! It is what it is. Just don't stick around and wait.

There is no substitute for time... don't waste yours.

...the COME ON STRONG MAN

T his feels good while it's happening. They show more than adequate interest, compliment you a lot and appropriately, want to spend time with you and make every effort to do so. It's nice, and you feel special, and almost relaxed because you don't have to wonder. The two of you make plans and talk a lot. You can tell that he wants to include you in his world. It's comforting and allows you to build trust. Then after the build up... BOOM!! They either say, *"I have to slow down, this is going too fast"*, or you hear nothing again... ever. They become the "NEVER CALL AGAIN MAN".

Again, takes about a month.

It makes me sad that so many people misrepresent themselves, both men and women. But, if one is not even aware that he or she has this issue... if this behavior is normal for them, I guess change is not on the horizon. But it can change for you! Don't sleep with him, no matter how nice he is... wait 90 days. You'll understand when you read the '90 day' guy.

We need to develop a 'people who misrepresent themselves detector', like a metal detector type of thing. Make them walk through it and if it goes off... you save a lot of time, just kick them to the curb.

See ya...

NEXT!!!!

...the I'M A FOREIGNER LIVING IN AMERICA MAN

Ok... if you live here, you play by the rules. I don't believe in diplomatic immunity when it comes to relationships. I grew up here, women vote here, and they can have careers. We are not baby machines or 'get you a drink while you sit there and do nothing' robots.

It's not ok to tell us what to do or for how long we can do it, and...

We don't have to check in with you before we make a decision, whether it's about a movie, a purchase, a friend, or an outfit.

Oh... and lose the attitude, it's not attractive.

And no, I am not wearing that thing on my head.

Yes, I know that American men act this way too. I am just trying to make a point.

...the **PROJECTOR MAN**

T his guy wears me out. *"I know you are, but what am I?"* is the motto. It's like being with a client constantly. Every issue that he has is just conveniently and miraculously yours.

You end up feeling like you are in the twilight zone or somewhere on another plane of consciousness. Or... like someone is playing a trick on you and it isn't very funny.

Before you know it, you really think there is a possibility that it might be you. These guys are very convincing because they wear you down ... and they never shut up, so you start to agree with them just so they will stop talking. I use this phrase now, *"are you still talking?"* when I am done with them. So, this doesn't happen to me anymore. I don't have the time or the patients... I mean patience. Ha Ha!

Remember.

It's not you.

If it feels weird, it probably is weird.

Follow your intuition in these cases. There is a diagnosis for this... but this is not that kind of book.

It's not your responsibility to convince them it's not you, either. It's just your responsibility to be aware, that's all, and decide what to do with that awareness.

i.e. Go to your therapist or leave town.

...the MIXED MESSAGE MAN

Here we go again. He loves me. He loves me not. I am telling you. I just don't have time for this anymore. What is the big decision making process here? You either like me, or you don't. You find me attractive, or you don't. You want to get to know me better, or you don't. So, how does "I'll call you tomorrow," turn into next month, year, or never?

And what is this calling every day to just talk? Do you think we don't notice that you don't want to get together? Why stay connected at all, unless, of course, you want a 'home base', a 'just in case girl', or the 'bootie call' girl?

A friend of mine was telling me about a guy that she has had this on-again-off-again thing with. They have been hanging out a lot lately and spending a good bit of time together. In addition, they have gotten a little intimate, so she asked where he thought it was going... what does he say? *"I don't want to have a girlfriend"*.

He wants all the fringe benefits, with no accountability.

Surprise!

Bottom line, when a man says he doesn't want to be in a relationship, he doesn't want to be in a relationship. And, it's called inconsistent reinforcement. Sometimes he likes you and sometimes he doesn't care. It keeps you there longer because it's unpredictable. Maybe, just maybe, this time... makes you search for ways to be hopeful.

I am hopeful that it will rain tomorrow.

So I don't have to cut my grass.

...the GIMME ANOTHER CHANCE MAN

Y ou know what I'm talking about.

He swears that he'll do better this time. He won't lie, cheat, steal or do whatever it was that he did... again. Otherwise known as the "can't decide" guy. blah blah blah... maybe this time.

If I wanted to play games, **Monopoly** is in my closet, so is **Clue**... maybe he should get one.

Have you heard any of these epiphanies?

> *"I realize what I had and I will never mess up again"*
>
> *"I'll do anything" (my personal favorite)*
>
> *"I just wasn't ready"*
>
> *"The timing was off"*
>
> *"If I can't make it with you, who else could I make it with?"*
>
> *"I had to grow up"*
>
> *"You are the one, honey, I swear. I just had to make sure"*

Yeah, thanks. Thanks for making *sure*. I am just so sorry, but... I am *sure* that I would need a legal document at this point.

I guess the positive side is that when you break up and get back together, they do things for you... like cut your grass. Then there is make up sex. Sometimes that's worth it; just use a condom (you don't know where he's been).

I think that when you don't care as much, they are more willing to make an investment. Maybe it's because they are still challenged and working at it. Once they realize that they have you, the task is complete and they can move on. So if they end up with someone who is more work than you were, they want you back. So don't spoil them. Be confident in your own decisions about what is ok with you. Go out with your friends. Only allow yourself to be thoughtful once in a while. Don't always make yourself available.

Let him work at pleasing you. It's not a game, it's a test, and he's taking it, not you. Also, it's not so much about whether he likes you, it's about if you like and wish to be with him. We seem to have forgotten this with all of our independence and education.

This is the class I needed in college. Maybe I should teach it now.

Just remember, first time, shame on him... second time shame on you. Sometimes, it's just too little, too late.

Another thing... Is he the guy that you want, or just the guy that you are with because you don't want to be alone?

...the HAS A 100 KIDS MAN

I am so sorry, but... no.

I love kids and I am quite open to the whole blended family thing, but come on. I just wonder where I fit in?

Is there really time for me?

One has a soccer game. Another has a recital, and so on and so on. Then there is the ex wife... holy heck! I just can't take it!!!

He doesn't have a family. He has a team... a tribe or something, and a very expensive one, at that.

There go my trips to Aspen.

But he's crazy if he thinks I'm giving up my Porsche.

...the NEWLY DIVORCED MAN

T his is the guy who is interviewing for his next wife.

I'll tell you, once they have been married many of them want to be married again.

Can't blame them, really. I liked being married. I just needed to learn how to make better choices.

Well, basically, I needed to have my head examined, which I did, and luckily no lobotomy was involved.

Anyway, these men aren't so bad. They are just at the other extreme. They want to move a little too fast, and have you moved in and walking the dog before you know what happened. Moving that fast in a relationship is always a risk. Unfortunately, the odds aren't in your favor.

The answer... set your boundaries.

Don't go to the next step, until you are ready. If he can't wait, or gives you a million reasons why this information is inaccurate, he probably is desperately looking for someone to fold his socks... or his kid's socks.

Oh, well, you see?

Issues with his mom...

i.e. He wants one!

...the GOOD LIAR MAN

Oh, dear, dear, dear... boy do I have a lot of information floating around in my head about this guy. We love to share with each other about this one, don't we? The stories never end, and there are so many different forms of dishonesty:

Lying by omission

Cheating

Manipulating

Avoiding

Pretending

Inconsistence

Blatant, outward, deceit

Loud and disrespectful

No follow-thru

Playing games

No matter what the form, the outcome is still the same, agonizing thing. So why, oh why, do we want to believe him so badly. What is it?

Well, sometimes it's charm, endearingness, fear, hope, stubbornness, money, promises, promises, promises... rationalization of promises, laziness, great sex... rationalization of great sex. They can be so alluring and mysterious.

Can you tell I'm ovulating?

Anyway, you will find yourself praying for some kind of follow-thru, or answer, until it consumes you.

Talk about issues with mom... hell, this is about the whole family vortex!

Here's a good story. Hopefully, my girlfriend will still talk to me after she knows I put this story in here. Ok, here it goes...

Girl meets guy at church.

Guy is a doctor.

Guy has lots of money, which he is obsessed with.

They date.

She catches him with another girl at his house.

She forgives him.

They date more.

He makes lots of promises.

He has the follow-thru of a gnat.

They do this for years

...and lots of jewelry

...and inappropriate behavior.

They break up and get back together a few times

Now he has even more money

She finds a hair clip on the nightstand... not hers

He swears it's the maid's... (sure it is)

She leaves.

She comes back after he begs and promises.

She finds a feminine product under the bed (dog finds it)... not hers.

She leaves.

He begs and buys himself more stuff to show her.

Doesn't buy her stuff, bad move.

She sees picture of him in paper with another woman.

He says they are just friends... and so on.

Get the picture..? 6 years of this! And she is beautiful and successful.

But, I have met this guy and he is a charmer. He comes across really humble. His other name is the F.O.S. MAN.

(F.O.S. means full of shit, for those interested.)

Don't trust the untrustworthy...

...the MAMA'S BOY MAN

Ugh!!!! This is why mothers-in-law get a bad name.

Can ya use the bathroom without asking her first? And, how many times a day do you need to talk to your mom? Why is her opinion the word of the highest power in the land? Why don't you know how to wash your own clothes, and why is it my job to cook all the time? You can run a company, but have to check with mom before you go away for the weekend?

Are these guys under a spell or something?

Wake up!

It's not attractive.

I dated a guy once whose mom called my house to check on him. She used to tell me that he wasn't like other "boys". He was special, and had special needs. Oh, he had special needs all right.

Another mother told me that I'd better be good in bed because that was the only thing that could keep him. Nice, huh? Where do people come up with this crap?

And... why the hell do they say it out loud?

...the RATIONALIZER MAN

These guys think that one good deed gets you off the hook for a bunch of bad ones. So he doesn't call for three weeks and forgets your birthday... doesn't matter, because, you see, he brought you flowers a-a-a-n-n-d-d gave you a card with a mushy message. So, I guess, that makes up for it, in his pea-brained, penis driven mind.

Or, maybe he cheated and rationalized it with the 'I was drunk' excuse. So... he couldn't be that responsible for his actions. He will only accept 20% of the responsibility, because, you know, he didn't really know what he was doing. What, did he have a speech impediment? Whatever. I say no trade offs. If you screw up, be a man and take ownership... and that includes your penis.

This also goes for the bad disposition. I always say that you can have anything that you want in this lifetime. It's all in your approach. If your approach stinks, your results probably will too. Don't you just hate the guy in the mall, who yells like some kind of nut because the salesperson didn't give him the answer that he wanted? I always feel sorry for the woman standing with him. What is she supposed to do? Laugh it off? Walk away? Yell at him? His rationalization is usually that it's someone else's fault, whether it be the salesperson, or the woman with him, or his dog, for that matter. Sounds like a personal problem to me.

Is hanging out with him worth the embarrassment? I personally, hate that kind of behavior, and I really resent the implication that I should accept it. So, I don't. I walk away and lose his number... and block mine.

...the 'BS' ARTIST MAN

Now this is different from the 'good liar' man because it is about closing the deal.

This is the guy who can con anyone.

He is the ultimate sales guy.

You want to believe everything he says even though that little voice in your head is saying... F.O.S., F.O.S.....alert, alert!

He will stop at nothing.

It takes about a month. Remember?

He'll start tripping over himself and his stories, in about a month... hopefully.

Either that or his follow-thru will give him away, because he will have none.

...the LOVES TO HEAR HIMSELF TALK MAN

I have one word for this, ANNOYING.

He should be called "ANNOYING MAN". They talk too much and say nothing. They use phrases to try to be funny or to try to make themselves sound smart. If you have to make yourself sound intelligent, you probably aren't intelligent.

There are two types.

Type One is the overconfident, egocentric, only talks about himself, and never includes you in the conversation.

He first, gives a sales pitch, and then, gives the dissertation to back it up.

Enough already,

I have a nail appointment.

Type Two I call the cobra.

He comes at you with challenging questions to try to "catch you off guard" or "catch you in a contradiction" to prove that he's listening or something.

He should be called the "MANIC MAN", because that's how I feel when it's over. When it, finally, is over.

I am not up for the competition, especially with someone that I am supposedly dating.

It all just gives me a headache.

Beware, these guys appear to be innocent, but appearances can be deceiving.

...the CHALLENGE ADDICT MAN

I t goes something like this...

A. He gets you

B. He leaves you

Next!!!

He only likes the infatuation. He doesn't like the building of the relationship, because he *isn't relationship material.*

Pay attention. He just wants you to think you are Cinderella.

It's your job to know that it is all fantasy. That's the reflection. He likes the fantasy of the challenge and you like the fantasy to come true.

Always a bad combination.

P.S. there is no white horse... sorry.

...the 90 DAY MAN

I have mentioned this already, but I haven't explained it.

I have dated a few guys like this, but my girlfriend dated a guy who actually said it out loud.

He basically gave her a countdown. There were gifts, nice dinners, double dates, quiet nights at home, sleepovers, and trips.

It all seemed to be going so well, until the third month. I guess that's the time where one could admit to oneself that there could be a relationship brewing. And so the sabotage begins.

Conveniently, it won't be his fault. It will probably be yours, because you ask too many questions, or nag all of a sudden, or want to be around all the time, or expect a phone call. Yet, these were all normal things... and cute, just a few days ago, because it was his idea.

Yeah, I know, it takes about a month... but it had so much potential. I ask you... do you have time for potential? Or do you want the real thing? Behaviors should match feelings.

You guessed it... issues with mom, a sister, aunts, first girlfriend, an ex-girlfriend... hell, women in general.

He's a big insecurity problem with a dash too much of control.

...the TRY TO BUY YA MAN

I don't have much experience with this guy, because most of the guys I have dated and married didn't have jobs.

I am halfway kidding.

All of you who know me are laughing.

Settle down.

It's nice to be wined and dined. It's nice to go shopping and not have to pay. It feels like Christmas or something. Trips are fun too, when you can just sit back and enjoy, or so I've heard.

But... these things, and money in general, do not replace inappropriate behavior.

Money does not erase or eradicate, meanness, rudeness, lack of social skills, cheating, bad punctuality, not showing up, not being available with time, emotional unavailability, general stupid behavior, being bad in bed, or bad teeth.

Show me... give me a reason to believe that you are a nice person.

You might have a nice car...but so do I.

...the SEX OBSESSED MAN

I said sex, not sexy. To him, sex is not a mutual experience, although he may give you the illusion that it is, because it starts out that way. It is a mission... an accomplishment.

At first, before the red flag goes up, you might think... "Wow, he's really open and into me". He takes his time and tries to please you and takes pride in the whole experience. This is nice, even if he fesses up to wanting just sex and nothing else. At least he's not pathological.

But...

...when it becomes obsessive, and he has to escalate his 'openness', and try to get you to do things that aren't comfortable, the flags should fly. It's a problem, especially if he tries to make you feel bad if you don't want to do something that he wants you to do.

Hanging off a chandelier or two is one thing, but supporting someone's fetish is another.

Remember, if it feels weird, it probably is weird. Don't do anything that you don't want to do, or that hurts, or that you aren't curious about. Also, just because you try something that you are curious about, doesn't mean you have to do it again, if you didn't like it. We are all individuals with likes and dislikes. If some sexual act is a deal breaker for him, let him go. It's not worth your self-esteem, and it certainly isn't worth him.

Sorry, I couldn't think of anything funny for this one, and sometimes I really do sound like a therapist.

I don't dress like one, though.

...the BORING MAN

He talks a lot about himself.

He calls to tell you about his day.

He tells you about his problems.

He asks you to wake him up in the morning.

He takes you to the restaurants that he likes.

He hangs out with his friends.

He likes to double date with couples that he knows.

He tells you what he wants for dinner,

He tells you what he wants in bed.

He doesn't care if you have an orgasm.

He asks you how he looks.

He waits for you to wash clothes.

He eats your groceries.

He takes you out when he wants to go out.

He buys you presents that he wants.

He waits for you to pick up the wet towel.

He waits for you to empty the dishwasher.

He asks you to pick up his dry cleaning.

He 'lets' you to walk his dog.

He wants you to be his maid, his therapist, his mom, his bud.

Asleep yet?

Dude!   What's in it for me?

...the **WHY DO YOU NEED YOUR OWN LIFE MAN**

I need my own life because I have a brain.

Find yours.

You have obviously left it somewhere... careful, don't look down.

...the HAS TO STAY IN TOUCH WITH HIS EX-GIRLFRIENDS MAN

When he remembers his ex-girlfriend's birthday and not yours, walk away.

When he gets her a better Christmas present than you, because he is making up for lost time, walk away.

When he has a standing appointment with an ex, once a month, on a Friday night, without checking with you first, walk away.

When he turns off his cell phone for substantial, and undisclosed periods of time, walk away.

Last, but not least...

If he lives with his ex-girlfriend, run away (very fast).

There is no sense talking about it and trying to make him understand why it isn't ok. He knows. It isn't rocket science. It's common sense, and men have common sense. They just pretend that they don't.

If he participates in these things, it's because he is keeping the doors open. There are lots of different types of doors: sliding, revolving, French, wood, glass, tall, short, half, whole... get my drift.

Variety is nice, when it is established that you are free to date whomever, whenever, wherever. Otherwise, it's just mean. Don't be the 'right now girl', unless, of course, he is doing other things to rock your world... and it's worth it to you. It is what it is.

Remember, reality, not fantasy.

...the **PROFESSIONAL BACHELOR MAN**

H^e does what he wants, when he wants, how he wants. Discussion is limited. He knows what he needs to get by, and has being with a woman down to a science. At first, his confidence is attractive and he can really play the game, without you knowing it's a game. He will tell you all the right things, such as:

> We are going to have so much fun because we have so much in common.
>
> I love weddings.
>
> I love animals.
>
> You are so pretty in the morning.
>
> When do I get to see you?
>
> Let me cook you dinner.
>
> I'll be there for you.
>
> I love hearing your voice on my voice-mail.
>
> I am very easygoing... not much offends me.
>
> I am so glad that I have someone to do things with.
>
> Hey, it's me.
>
> When can I meet your brother... father... mom?
>
> What do you want to do this weekend?
>
> I'll call you tomorrow.
>
> I'll check in later.
>
> How was your day?
>
> I want to learn everything about you.
>
> What will you do when I fall in love with you?
>
> What do you want for Christmas?

Can I cut your grass?

Blah, blah, blah. You are probably saying that even guys with good intentions say these things. That is true. I'm not talking about those guys. The professional bachelor guy is who I'm talking about and he just has really good timing. He seems to know what you are thinking, and more importantly, what you want to hear, and when you want to hear it. He can be the "pretend man", the "monogamously challenged man", the "challenge addict" the "never calls again guy", the "commitment phobic" or any combination... etc.

Remember what he "says", and what he "does" won't match. Here's what he **won't** really do:

Go to weddings with you.

Spend the whole night.

Tell you where he is.

Tell you who he is with.

Spend long periods of time with you... like a whole day, unless it's a weekend out of town and he can't escape.

Pay for everything.

Make plans before Thursday.

Commit to an event more than a week away.

Introduce you to his friends.

Take you to work functions.

Give you his home phone number.

Take you on normal dates.

Follow thru.

Fall in love with you.

Get you a Christmas gift

Cut your grass!

His life is his life, and yours is yours. The good thing is, that he doesn't really bother you much. The bad thing is, that it gets boring, especially if you don't know if you are in an exclusive thing or not... even when you ask. If you can't get a straight answer... what do you do? Wait it out? Forget it. I don't have time for potential. This just has the potential to get on my nerves.

The professional bachelor has one big flaw that gives him away.

His behaviors won't match his feelings. A dead giveaway.

Takes about a month.

The attractive confidence is a mask for fear of attachment.

No real mystery there.

Secret message received.

...the THINKS HE IS OVER EDUCATED MAN

This cracks me up. Men say they like an intelligent, balanced woman, until they come across one. Then they act like a deer in headlights. You would think that a man who is 'educated' or career minded would be comfortable with a woman who is the same. Well, apparently not. I guess they think they can get away with more or don't have to be as 'on their toes' if they don't perceive you as intelligent or as ' together' as they appear to be. Then you find out they live with their parents.

I dated an attorney once, who said that he didn't care if his girlfriend worked, but if he married her, he wanted her to stay at home. It didn't matter if they had kids or not, he just didn't want to risk her making more money than him. It's too hard to explain, he said. He felt that roles needed to be clearly defined. Yeah, right... so if he felt that his role was to have an affair, her role would be to stick around and be the cook, maid, and nanny. That's how it sounds to me, anyway. I still can't believe I hear this stuff out loud. Don't they know that people write books?

How about the guy who has to boast about how successful he is?

What is up with that?

He's the one who laughs out loud when you tell him what you do, so he can make a condescending remark.

"Oh, you're a therapist... what kind? I don't believe in that stuff. Who pays to talk to somebody about their crap? I can't believe people go to school for that!"

Well, you obviously don't own that book on how to be a gentleman. Maybe you should go to school for that.

...the WHY DO YOU HAVE TO SPEND TIME WITH YOUR FAMILY MAN

I have to spend time with my family because they are my family and they are not dead. It's simple. If you are lucky enough to still have your parents, not only alive, but together, you go and see them on occasion. Sometimes it's a birthday, other times it's a holiday and still other times there is no reason... you just want to.

I was married to a guy who said that there was absolutely no reason to see your family more than twice per year. Well, if I had his family, I wouldn't want to see them once per year. So, I saw his point, it just didn't apply to me.

If I were to write a book on a guy with mom issues, his picture would be on the cover... front and back.

No love lost there.

...the JESUS MAN

Ahhhh... the religious hypocrite. He preaches the word of God... till Friday and Saturday night. Those are the nights, you see, he parties till dawn... but it's ok, because he goes to church on Sunday to clean the slate. It's the new Blank Slate theory. Then all is well till the next week. And premarital sex... for some reason, those church type rules about sex and stuff don't apply to him. I don't know how he got exempt, but I guess he did. Maybe he was a saint in his last life, or the Pope, or maybe an Egyptian God. Who knows.

Here's the part that bugs me. "So Sonia, did you go to church on Sunday? Why not? You should go to church." Well, I don't have as much to repent, number one. Number two, it's none of your business how I worship. Number three, don't tell me how you went to a party where there were a bunch of strippers, got drunk, and slept in someone's hallway (like I buy that anyway) and then got your ass up and went to church. Give me a break... good thing God does, cause I don't. Pass the aspirin over here... I'm the one with the headache.

And, P. (frickin) S.... people like this, they lack integrity. Jesus had integrity. But, choose to forgive them. Things can only affect you if you allow them to affect you. Sometimes, they grow out of this stupid behavior and genuinely feel bad about it. I don't know if I would stick around to find out, though.

Be Healed!

Oh, and P. (frickin) S. is P.S. with (frickin) in the middle.

...the 4 MINUTE MAN

I looked at the clock at 11:04, and it was over at 11:08. Hell, I had nothing else to do. No foreplay, no orgasm, no kidding. Now... why in the world would a man assume that you were satisfied, when it's over in four minutes? I can't even fake it that fast. How is that even possible? It isn't, even with alcohol. So, I guess it means he doesn't really care. (Ya think?) As long as he gets what he needs, it's rated as a successful experience... for him. He never even asked if I was, well, alive.

Whew who!! Can't wait till next time. Maybe it'll last 5 minutes!

A. He needs the book on how to be a gentleman.

B. He needs to learn the mind, body experience concept.

C. He needs to learn a **Woman's Anatomy**.

D. He needs to learn a little about control.

E. He needs to cut my grass.

Selfish, selfish, selfish

Onward and upward my friends.

...the MALE CHAUVINIST MAN

R efer to the 'men are pigs' comment earlier in the book.

Don't be afraid because we may be smarter, more talented and more resilient than you...

Embrace it...

Then go to therapy... and then buy the book on how to be a gentleman... who learns to like women.

...the RECOVERY EVANGELIST MAN

T his is the guy in AA or NA or Al-anon or any other 12 step program. First, let me say that I have gone to Al-anon for years. The 12 steps saved my proverbial butt. It is the only reason that I am thankful for my first husband. The only reason.

But, I don't need every, solitary, second of my life critiqued. Stop!!!! Don't take my inventory... focus on your own. I totally respect the 12 steps and traditions, but I like figuring it out for myself. I don't need a 30-minute explanation on how I shouldn't use artificial sweeteners (I don't know why, I don't remember what the explanation was.), or how I should get up earlier, or how I should go to more meetings or how my family is codependent. It's my choice, and I know my family is codependent. Don't preach to me... or my friends... or my pets etc.

It takes a while to find a balance... call me when you calm down or when your Prozac kicks in.

...the NEVER HAS MONEY MAN

Oh please. I'll bet you have money to go out drinking with your buds, or for Braves, Hawks, or Falcons tickets. And... it's just amazing to me, how there is always money just laying around for a new mountain bike, or some hunting equipment... but not enough to take us out for a nice dinner once in a while. Hell, I want a new bike. I'm not into hunting, but I like to shoot skeet. Anyway...

And, why is it assumed that I am willing to cook several times a week, because, you know, I don't have a life. And, I go to that free grocery store. You know the one... where they just give food away and you don't have to pay for it.

So... let's talk priorities, shall we? Are you a priority? Or are you an extracurricular activity. I am not an extra anything. I am the real thing. If he doesn't get that, he doesn't get me.

And stop buying the coffee at Starbucks all the time.

...the ARTIST

Not the 'artist' man, just the 'artist'.

Ahhh, the sacrifice is overwhelming. It has to be difficult, and it has to involve drama... and he has to leave... for the sake of love. He has to sacrifice everything for his art.

The art of being an idiot.

No wonder artists hardly ever become famous until they are dead.

...the WORKAHOLIC MAN

My girlfriend dates a guy that she can only see once per month. Now, if you have the chance to see a woman that you like and possibly could be having sex with, wouldn't you find a way to "get off" early. I mean, who is he? The president? I don't think so.

When a man wants to be with a woman, wild horses can't keep him away... and neither can his job, nor his ex wife, or his kids, or his other miscellaneous responsibilities. We all have miscellaneous responsibilities.

These guys give a very clear message. They don't want to make time. Why? I don't know. They may not like you enough. They may not be good communicators, they may not multi task well, they may be immature, they may be monogamously challenged, they may be married. They may not be for you.

There are other fish in the sea... so cast another line or two, and use different bait.

...the **MARRIED 100 TIMES MAN**

Y ou have to wonder, don't you? Is he the male version of Elizabeth Taylor, or what?

Go to therapy already, and figure it out. It's a lot cheaper and far more effective. It would mean... less alimony, less child support, less college tuition... and less therapy for less people. Make the commitment to yourself. Changing women does not change your issues.

...the OLDER MAN

There *may* be baggage, but there may be money.

...the YOUNGER MAN

There *may* be less baggage, but probably no money.

Well, as Ivana Trump says, "Do you want to be a nurse, or a babysitter?"

So... who is more likely to cut my grass? That's who wins in my world.

...the RED NECK MAN

I am not sure if red neck is the appropriate term, but this is the guy who hates everybody. I guess he should be called the "hates everybody" guy. He doesn't like, old people, young people, black people, purple people, gay people, married people, smart people, slow people, Jewish people, people who don't drive trucks, people who drive red trucks... etc.

He has a crew-cut and a can for his tobacco spit. He only wears T-shirts and jeans with, of course, cowboy boots... hat optional. Although, usually, the hat is a baseball cap with a tractor on it.

How do you meet them? Not in a vegetarian restaurant, that's for sure. Sometimes it's in the Kroger (grocery store), and other times at the little Mexican place over a pitcher of margaritas... well, there you go. Seems ok at the time, until you sober up.

...the A.D.D. MAN

C an you say... pin ball in a pin ball machine? I can't follow his conversation, his voicemail, his trail...

How about bringing it down a notch or two? Speak slowly and clearly into the phone... and keep your arms and hands in the vehicle and away from the door (That's what the voice says on the tram at the Atlanta airport).

FOCUS! I'M OVER HERE!

And don't stop till I tell you to...

...the HIGH MAINTENANCE MAN

This guy just can't get it right. He needs constant and consistent reinforcement. Is this ok? Is that ok? Are you ok? Is the dog ok? Ok already. We are ALL ok. Relax. I need anti anxiety meds by the end of the day.

Daily life functioning is an event for this dude. All in all, he just wants things to be perfect, and will go to great lengths to prevent mistakes and "non perfectness". Unfortunately, I can relate to this. Thank goodness for al-anon and therapy. It really helped my anal retentiveness, otherwise known as the 'control issue'.

It seems to be very harmless at first, even cute, that he is so concerned about you and everything around you. But, since striving for perfection just reinforces our inadequacies, it isn't long before his temper flares or objects start flying across the room. It's all or nothing, and extremes are never good. The outcome is... once again, it's not about you and his concern for you, it's about controlling his environment.

Psych 101 lesson: you can't control anything outside of yourself, you can only control you. Sort of like the reality/fantasy thing that I keep saying. Well, at least I quit with the "issues with mom" concept.

So... You can't control the outcome of this relationship, unless, of course, you dump him. Bummer.

...the WHY DO YOU NEED FRIENDS MAN

See the "why do you need your own life" guy. Again, I need to have other friends because I have a brain and sometimes it's boring to just be with you. This is especially true when I want to talk about you, or complain about you, to a girlfriend, over a martini. So go away for a while before I change the locks... or move.

...the SECRETIVE MAN

So.....where is he? Where does he work? Is he married? Does he have a girlfriend? Is he sleeping with other people? Did he go to college? Why doesn't he call? Does he have a house? Does he have kids? Why is he inconsistent? Etc. etc.

Sometimes men associate vulnerability with the loss of freedom, so they stick to minimal disclosure. I guess they think you'll either, not notice, or, just put up with it. Granted, you don't owe anyone an *explanation* for how you feel, but that doesn't mean that you shouldn't *express* how you feel. Two different things, explanation and expression. Explaining can be a way to rationalize and hide. Expressing can be a way to be emotionally available. Oooooh, sounds scary.

The reality of the situation is... if he seems secretive, he *is* secretive and that's just plain weird. Really, it's dishonest. What a great start to a friendship or relationship... weirdness and dishonesty. The fantasy in your mind is that you are Cinderella. Unfortunately, the Cinderella story is the *exception*, not the rule. I don't know about you, but I am the exception to enough rules.

Again, there is no white horse.

...the CAN'T DECIDE MAN

Come on, get it together, for God's sake. Make a decision.

Here we go with the big decision making process again. They can't decide if they like you or not. They can't decide if they think you are hot enough or not. They can't decide if your boobs are big enough. They can't decide if you are worth a nice restaurant, or just lunch. They can't decide what shirt to wear or whether or not they should take a shower. Should I go work out? Or should I go have a beer? Should I try to sleep with Angela? Or Rebecca? Or maybe both... at the same time! For heaven's sake, these are not life changing events. Just deal.

No woman likes being second choice... or third or forth, for that matter. Our mistake as women is that we accept something instead of nothing. Remember. It's about whether *you* like him. You are administering the test that he is taking. And for the record... it isn't your job to correct his answers, and try to make him into what you want or think he should be. It was cheating in school, and it is cheating now.

And, by the way dudes, don't ask someone to spend time with you if you are going to cancel at the last minute. "I'd really like to go to dinner, but I got this opportunity to go fishing" or "You don't mind if I pick up a shift, I need the money", after I have gone grocery shopping and gotten off work early myself. Aside from being hurtful, it's just inconsiderate. I don't like feeling like my time is not important. I get paid for my time. So, to me, that is the ultimate rudeness, not to mention that it's invalidating, and juvenile. I am trying to say that it's not a smart way to make a good impression. But then, if it were about a good impression, we wouldn't be having this discussion.

...the MAN WHO TAKES HOSTAGES

T his is the guy who makes up the rules as he goes. Why does this happen? It happens because we don't like making choices ourselves. So, we take a rest for a while, and let someone else do it. Then we wake up and oops.... a whole bunch of really bad choices have been made for us and we were asleep the whole time. Imagine that. It's as simple as paying attention. Relationship dynamics can get out of control sometimes, if we don't pay attention.

My girlfriend, who is also a therapist, has been dating this guy for two years. When they talk about getting married, it's always this big dilemma. He wants her to give up her career to be married to him. Yet, he was attracted to her because of her independence and drive to be self-sufficient. Anyway, she wants to continue to build what she has worked on for so long. She has just completed her PhD., for God's sake. Now she is in private practice and is doing well. But... she made allowances. She moved in with him, but still pays for her place. She follows his rules of his household. She fell into his family system, even though she has her own education and her own life and her own home. She follows his rules. To top it off, he is rich. But... does he help her with her bills? No. Does he offer to help her to be more financially comfortable? No. Does he try to show her how wonderful it would be to be married to him? No. So why should she offer herself? He is offering her no security at all. He is just holding her hostage.

Now, this is a guy who has had a drinking problem (untreated by the way). Yet, he is making the rules... and I thought that Psychologists had good testing skills (Get it? She should be giving the test!! Pay attention!). Oh well. So, he tells her that this is the way it's going to be.

Man....he would have my foot so far up his butt that his eyes would poke out. But, I am Italian, after all. Comes with the territory.

The bottom line is, that he is very insecure and preys on other's insecurities. He knows he isn't good enough for her. Remember, we seek out in other's what we see in ourselves. My friend has finally told him that she is not afraid of being alone. She is afraid to be with him. Bravo.

I just don't have time to let this crap rent space in my head. He should be ashamed of himself for trying to 'cage' people in his world, instead of looking at himself.

So, is it because we are afraid of making the wrong choice? Or is it because we don't want to take responsibility for any choice? I say, make the choice based on your own best interests. You are the only one who has to spend the rest of your life with you.

Relationships are supposed to be about fellowship, nurturing and unconditional love...not reflecting dysfunction. Although, it is how we must learn, sometimes.

...the ONE FOOT OUT THE DOOR MAN

This guy is a little different from the 'can't decide' guy or the 'commitment phobic' guy. He really plays the part... and for a long time. But, just when you think it's safe, he turns on you. It's almost like the relationship never happened. He's gone, sometimes physically, sometimes emotionally, sometimes, both. And, guess what? No explanation. No expression. No nothing. Weird, isn't it? I don't have a compartment in my head for this, and I don't think it's in my best interests to form one.

Maybe there is another girlfriend, or he is married. Maybe he just has attachment issues, which is usually caused by feelings of abandonment. It could be emotional abandonment by a parent. It could be physical abandonment by a parent. It could be narcissism, because the narcissist's biggest fear is abandonment. If you keep one foot out the door, you will never, technically, be abandoned. It could be fear of commitment, which could be about making the wrong decision. Keeping one foot out the door is a way to not make a decision. It could be bad communication skills. It hard to say things, such as: "I am scared to get married" or "can we just leave things alone" or "I think that it just isn't going to work, even though I want it to work" or "I can't be monogamous" or "you are bugging me". It could be selfishness. He just doesn't care enough any more and doesn't care to tell you. But... these are reasons, not excuses. There is no excuse for not being accountable. It's just lazy, inconsiderate, and an abusive way to be in or out of a relationship with someone, because it's dishonest.

...the INVISIBLE MAN

This is the guy who appears out of nowhere and disappears into nothingness. Sometimes he lives in another state, which makes it easier to be invisible. Other times he lives down the street and you wonder how he is so invisible. Either way, the inconsistence creates an *idea* to which you eventually can get attached. Another mind game.

Let's say you meet him in a restaurant while on vacation. Because time is limited, a lot happens all at once. He tells you that you are beautiful, that you hung the moon, that you will travel and take long weekends together. He claims and acts like he has lots of money. Wow! The whole damn package. No kids, no divorces... no marriages. Why hasn't he been married? "He just hasn't found the one who can make him settle down," he says. Right...

Next thing you know, he is visiting you and telling you that he's going to fall in love with you. He text messages like crazy. Then he doesn't call for a week. Why? He says he's been busy and on a business trip. But, he wants to get together soon. In fact, "Check some flights for this weekend," he says. "But," you say, "I am feeling uncomfortable with your mixed messages. It seems like you come on really strong, and then just disappear." Then he doesn't call again and the weekend passes. He finally calls. "Baby" he says, "Where's the love? Don't you think you are acting a little insecure? I mean, I've been busy! Come on... come and see me."

Hmmm. Now I see why he isn't in a relationship. He's part projector, part liar, part come-on-strong man, part pretend man, part professional bachelor, but basically, FOS. Remember what that means? It means that this "invisible" man is no superhero.

There's also the invisible man who makes plans and makes you wait, and wait, and wait. He has five million excuses and five million apologies. He also probably has a wife or a girlfriend...

When a man wants to be with you, wild horses can't keep him away. As I have said before, not having time for me, does not impress me.

Don't attach meaning to the *idea* of the man. Make sure the man is real.

...the DRAMA MAN

Ever date a guy who thinks his life is a movie? He is constantly running, breathing hard, hand on forehead. Drama, drama, drama. "I simply must do this NOW! It can't wait! Oh, my God! Answer the door! It might be the police! Help me! Please! Hurry!" It makes you feel like you should be looking for a camera in the bushes and cue cards across the street. Lights. Camera. Action!

See me running down the street, away from you! Make sure the camera gets that, because you only get one "take" and I don't need a cue card.

This guy must be really bored if he has to pretend to be in his own life.

Then there's the drama guy who always has drama around him. The ex girlfriend who won't let go or the ex wife that is seeking to destroy him, or the kids that need treatment for substance abuse, or the business partner that's stealing money. Make sure you check out whether he has the drama pathology or just attracts it. As a therapist, I have a little of both, but I can tell which is me and which is not. In reality, whether he attracts it because he is a "fixer" and thinks he can help everyone (instead of himself), or he is a part of it (meaning he "is it") is worth investigating. The first is much more "fixable" than the second. "Crazy makers" are not worth the trouble or the outcome. So, pretend you are Sherlock Holmes and do a little follow up or following.

...the ARE YOU A LESBIAN MAN

Yeah.....I'm a lesbian, because I don't like you. I would have to like girls if I didn't like you. You are just so perfect. No....you aren't narcissistic at all. Everyone should want you because you are just so hot. Right...it's your confidence I'm uncomfortable with. It's not that tick that you have, or the way you snort in public, or the fact that you wear too much self-tanner and color your hair a weird, unnatural color.

Maybe I should be a lesbian. Why...why, I ask, do I do this to myself?

...the BOOTIE CALL MAN

He calls, and you are there. He texts and you are there. You call and where is he? You text and... nothing. hmm mm. What's in it for you?

So, of course I am going to ask... does he cut your grass? Does he help you when you have a flat tire? Do you get dinner? A movie? A boob job? An orgasm?

Yeah, that's what I thought... get rid of him.

...the JEALOUS MAN

here are two types of jealous men. The first is the obvious. No matter where you go, he is wondering what you are doing and with whom. Is he so concerned because he isn't trustworthy? Or, is he so concerned because he is wildly insecure? Relationships are reflections, and I don't like reflecting either one of those things, or the stuff that goes along with it. Insecurity on crack, is how it all ends, with both people running in circles, playing search and destroy.

The other type of jealous man might be better named the "intimidated" man. He thinks you are really cool at first, because you are self-sufficient. For example, I started, and continue to run, my own business, I own property, I have an awesome car (I love my car), a house, an education, a good haircut, and I got it all myself... ex husbands not included. I want a partner to accentuate my life. The rest I am capable of doing on my own. I don't always like it, but I can handle it just fine.

Well, oops. I don't need him. Now he might have to be a true partner and be emotionally available. He can't use the, "Look at all that I do for you" rationale. That one is dead in the water with me. So, usually what happens is he says, "You know, I just don't know how to be in a relationship with you.". I'll tell you how.... cut my grass. I already told you that it rocks my world, and just because I can do stuff myself, doesn't mean I like it. For God's sake, didn't your mom and dad teach you to help people?

...the IN THE MOMENT MAN

This man is different from the "challenge addict" because he sticks around, as long as you let him. He could also be called the minimalist. He does just enough to get by, but gives the illusion that he does a lot. He claims to be private in nature, but really he's just secretive. He is usually not the monogamous type, hence the clandestine allure, but he is fun to talk to, good at lots of things, blah, blah, blah. The reality: he is only in it for the moment. The fantasy: he really wants you. Everything he says is true, it is just for the moment. That's the kicker. That's what draws you in, because he said you were beautiful... and that he couldn't wait to see you again... and that you were just so intriguing. It's probably true, and you probably are beautiful, and intriguing. He should want to see you again. Makes sense. Unfortunately, his moments change from one moment to the next, convenient only to him.

This is the last story. I am embarrassed about it, so I saved it for last. I met this guy at the gym. He works there...first mistake. We had some major chemistry, which doesn't happen often. I ignored it for a while, and then he got brave and initiated a friendship, which I knew was not what he was after. Well, remember the pretty boy issue I have? So, I succumbed. Second mistake. Then I find out (he doesn't tell me, or most people) there is this girl that he has been dating a while. Oops. I back off. His plate is too full and I don't like to get in the middle of that sandbox. Then... I date the "just too busy" guy, and at a vulnerable moment, find myself entertaining the "in the moment" guy again. Now, both choices are emotionally unavailable. So... why, you ask, do I partake? Well, the "just too busy" guy leaves you feeling dispensable and unimportant... so the "in the moment" guy fills in the gap. He gives you a little time, which is still not enough, but more than the last guy.

He tells you that he is so attracted to you...and that you make him nervous...and that he wants you. So you take door number one, the illusion door. The illusion that it's ok. Besides, it can get you over the hump. It's temporary. Then the hump becomes a mountain.

The mountain looks down into a pit of vulnerability... and you fall into it. He's still up there on the mountain, but doesn't even come half way down to help you. Not his moment, not his problem. But, he says he's thinking about you and hopes you are okay.

Here we are, back to accountability. The "in the moment" guy never has to be accountable. He just divides his life up. He is dad in one place, husband in another place, sex god over here, the great friend over there, and the nice reserved guy at work. He is like a chameleon (one of those lizards that changes color according to the situation). It should be obvious that *he* has too many gaps and that it would be in his best interests to work on them. His illusion is that it's all good, because each segment is separate and each of those segments is going just fine for him. So he continues to use different people to fill different holes in his life. See the 'gap' reflection? I had gaps and he had gaps. The gap I filled for him, created one for me. I felt dispensable and I allowed him to make me dispensable. In his world, the situation was adding value, but in my world, it was a devaluing mind game.

The problem with his theory is that you are always only one person. Who you are in your personal life is a direct reflection of who you are professionally, and visa versa. Luckily, I don't want to form a compartment in my head for this. I don't want to reflect this dysfunction, because, it is not who I am. I might get caught up, but I don't stay long. It made me feel insecure, unattractive, and completely unimportant. I wanted to run away. What does he say to me? "We are both strong enough to be friends, at the least. I care about you and I am thinking about you." And that, *my friends*, is supposed to fix it. He is thinking about me. He cares about me. What a prize. What's in it for me? Why would he think that I would want such an unreliable friend? How does that add value to my life? As far as I am concerned, it was just another conquest. He used the caring crap as a rationalization for his behavior, so I would be nice to him, and not make a scene.

Let me tell you...shame on me. I guess I had to feel it again.... That I am not a side dish, like broccoli. I hate broccoli. I am main course material. It's hurtful to be a conquest for someone. It makes you feel like broccoli.

To him I say it is not polite to use people to fill in the sections of your life that need work. Go to therapy. But, just know...I am thinking about you and I hope you are okay. Take care. Yeah, you know who you are. Your girlfriend should send me a thank you note.

Just for the record, he only cut my grass once, and only the back. I deserve more than a moment.

...the TOXIC MAN

I have 2 words...Toxic waste. Find a dump and leave it there.

Every single, solitary thing he does is toxic. It's way worse than the "projector" man. He's not just needy, he's really, really needy. He's not just angry, he's really really angry. Really, really jealous. Really, really perfectionistic. He has no filter in his communication style, so it's always about calming him down or making him more comfortable. It's called chaos management. So, the result of your efforts will be, your balance falling apart. Then you are both a little off, which does make him more comfortable. Plus, you will fit in with his family better when you are a little nuts too.

You can't make logic of an illogical situation (that's from AA). So, if you are spending a lot of time trying to figure him out and feeling sorry for him, ask yourself...what is your goal? Do you think you will fix him and he will be indebted to you for life? Not going to happen. If he gets fixed, he won't need you anymore... because you will be broken. But, chances are, he won't get fixed. Helping him is not going to make the two of you closer, either. That only happens in the movies. This is real life. Stand back and assess the situation. It doesn't matter how much time you have invested or how sorry you feel for him or how guilty he wants you to feel. Be realistic and honest with yourself. It's your life. You get what you deserve, but you determine what you deserve. So set your boundaries appropriately.

If you think about it, there is no way his intentions could be appropriate. No possible way. You know that way you look at someone, out of the corner of your eye, when you know they are a little off? You sort of cock your head to the side a little. Well, that's your cue. He needs a referral and some medication.

...the THOUGHTLESS MAN

Y ou wait, and wait, and wait, and wait...and wait.

Does he call? When he wants to. If he gets around to it. Does he spend time with you? If he has nothing else to do. If he isn't able to make other plans. Everything else is more important. So, you get left hanging on Friday night, and possibly Saturday too. I've had stalkers who were more desirable and at least willing to spend time with me.

The "thoughtless" man is the king, and I mean KING, of consistently being inconsistent. He keeps you on a string. If you talk to him about it, he is appropriate. He listens, but has little to say. He can't form a statement that quickly. Of course, communication isn't really his strong point. He's good at the "have a nice day" routine and the "how was the visit with your parents". Surface talk. Charming, but surface.

Sometimes these guys are good at nonverbal communication, like sex. At that point you can make your decision as to whether talking is really that important anyway. It usually is for me.

So, is this enough for you? No flowers, no dinners, no surprise lunches, no little notes or sweet phone calls... just a roll in the hay, every now and again. Unless, he asks for more... like if you can take care of his dog or give him a ride to the airport. It's all about him. He's like the "in the moment" man.

So here is what you do, and this is compliments of my girlfriend, who says that you "play cards". You have a hand and he is just one of the guys (cards) in your hand. That way, if he doesn't follow thru, there is always another one close by. You can't take these guys really seriously, because that's not how they operate. They are playing cards too.

What she is really saying is to pay attention to the reality of the situation (which is that he is unreliable, inconsistent, not dependable, but cute) not the fantasy in your mind (that he is nice, upstanding, and relationship material). Oh, and make sure none of his other girlfriends are pregnant, and if so, you know what hand she is playing.

...the ONE DAY AT A TIME MAN

T his has nothing to do with the program of recovery and the 12 steps.

This has to do with the guy that you meet and have this great connection with. At least you think there is a mutual connection... he acts like there is a mutual connection. For those of us that don't date a lot or have a "hand of cards" this seems more real than it is. As a normal human woman, you form an attachment to it. We all want to belong...not to someone, but *with* someone. It seems like this guy could be a possibility. They are all possibilities, after all. So... you tell him. You put yourself in a vulnerable position, and you tell him that you really enjoy spending time with him and you really want to see him again. That's what mature women do. We put it out there...so we can get answers and move on. He says... "Well, you know, I just take things one day at a time." He doesn't say that he wants to see you again. He doesn't seem overtly concerned when you leave. He doesn't make a plan or give you any indication that you are becoming a staple in his life. But...when you are with him, he is so nice and so sincere. You feel like a princess and it's very fun and comfortable and relaxed. How could he not want to see you again? He *acts* like he is really into you.

Do his behaviors match his feelings?

Hmmmmm.

It's confusing.

He sends emails and calls pretty regularly. Of course, you are waiting for any attempt at communication... which puts you in a space of settling for less than you deserve. But he is always just too, too busy. Yeah, I've heard that before. The Just Too Busy Man.

Again... too busy for what? Not having time for me does not impress me.

It's hard to move on.

So at first, you do the waiting game. Maybe he is shy, or just got out of a relationship (where he really got hurt), maybe he had a bad divorce, maybe he has money issues, maybe he has chronic pain, maybe his job is stressful, maybe he has issues with his mom.... or he's scared. Blah, blah...blah blah. Here's what I say... Whaaaaaaa. We all have some of those issues. It's part of being an adult. You either step up to the plate, or you don't.

It's hard to move on.

My bottom line is this: The human spirit needs unconditional love, acceptance and truth. It needs compassion and a sense of belonging. We crave it and we look for it. These guys do too, but they (like so many other warning label guys) are too clueless to know that they don't know! So you are beating your head against the wall... waiting. They only change if they want to change, or recognize that they could, for heaven sakes. When your soul... his soul... your parent's souls... your sibling's souls open up to be nourished, they can be nourished. Otherwise you are trying to get someone who is used to junk food, to want, crave, and enjoy, organic food.

It takes a lot of honesty and willingness to allow your soul to open up. Fact is, your soul might already be more open, making it harder to move on without waiting to make sure... that his soul is truly closed to any new business.

Follow your path, but know when to say when.

...the YOU ARE JUST TOO DIFFICULT MAN

H igh maintenance means high quality.

I am tired of men telling me that I am just too difficult or that they don't know how to deal with me.

Why?

Because I am not easily manipulated... which I am, as seen in several of my stories.

Well, when I have my head together it's a different scenario. Then, I am difficult... high maintenance. I hear phrases like, *"No matter what I do, it's not good enough"* or *"You are always telling me what I am doing wrong"* or *"You are so uncomfortable with so many things"*.

I realize that part of this belongs to me, and that I am responsible for my part. But, if I try to take responsibility for the parts that belong to me and I still hear these phrases, I end the conversation. They probably aren't good enough, and they aren't doing things appropriately and they are making me uncomfortable. They don't know, that they don't know. We are high maintenance because they don't want to do the right thing. It's too difficult, it takes too much thought and.... their *fear* is stronger than their *desire* to change. That means one very important thing.

We, my friends, will never be a priority.

These men will *wait* for life to happen to them.

They don't *make* life happen to them.

I create my own reality and then let things fall into place, not the other way around. I like to make my own decisions, and again, I want a partner to help me with that. I don't want decisions to *happen* to me.

When a guy says to you, *"You never know what's going to happen"*, or *"You just may be the one"*, or *"things may change"*.

Blah, blah, blah.

Those phrases mean that you really do know what's going to happen. Nothing.

He is comfortable with things the way they are, so why think ahead. It's pointless *for him* to think ahead, but it's going to be tragic *for you* not to think ahead.

Years will go by, and you will still be seeing the guy with the live-in girlfriend (because she gives him buddy airline passes to see his kids).

So there you are... waiting for it to be convenient for him to steal a few hours here and there. What's in it for you?

Diamonds?

Lawn service?

Yeah, I doubt it.

You are supposed to be happy with what you can get, because it's better than nothing and you have nothing else going on. Right? WRONG!! You will never find "something" if you are busy and focused on the "nothing" because "nothing" makes you feel like crap. And why would "something" be interested in crap?

Don't feel bad... I've done it too.

Again, I am not broccoli.

Are you?

...the SHOPPER

T his is the guy who already has a girl that he dates. He was in a relationship with her, but now he just dates her. He is open to dating other people. Does she know this... probably not? He tried to break up with her, but she wouldn't take no for an answer. Since there was no one else around at the time...he just keeps on keeping on. Convenient, yes... ethical, no. But it works, till he meets the next one. Till then, he shops. In girl language, it's like buying a dress and leaving the tag on till your sure, so you can return it. In guy language, it's like leasing a car and turning it in before it has too many miles on it... or the new model is just too much to let slip by.

So, when you meet him, you are the instant consolation prize. He just wants to "try it out" to, you know, "see if it fits".

He'll take you out on a first date which is actually a date (not a hang out session)... the "hook you in date". I know you all know what I am talking about. He'll act like he wants to know everything about you and that you are so cool, have so much in common and...you are just what he wants. Funny how they can, all of a sudden, remember the "little things", like sitting right next to you and holding your hand... complimenting you in front of the server and... paying for dinner. Men know what they have to do to impress you and it doesn't take long... about an hour, really. So, a little bit of time later, after you are thinking that he could actually be a nice guy and you see the potential in this person, the truth comes out. It takes about a month to know a man, remember? But if your good.... it takes less and less time.

Anyway, you hear the "girlfriend" word. And you realize... he's not just dating her. There is a history.

Then, of course, you get demoted (after you start asking questions about the other girl thing). You then become the "frrriiiennd". That way he can shop you and still be with her. See, you are the cool girl until you start asking questions.

In his reality, nothing has to change until he is sure he can give up the other one… then maybe you can get picked. Yippie… until he does the same thing to you. It's disrespectful and thoughtless to both people. And you know why men do this? Because we, as women, have allowed it. This guy could not believe it when I said that I didn't want to continue this little "get to know you session". I knew all I needed to know. So he tried to push it off on me…like I was too difficult and making a big deal out of nothing. Well, if it's nothing, why are you calling me every day? Blah, blah, blah. Dork.

Well, newsflash… dude… I don't want to be your friend. All of a sudden we have to be friends first. All of a sudden it's so important that we move really slow. Yeah, I was born yesterday. (I wish I were born in the 80's actually).

Why, I ask, is this necessary? Just be a man and break up with the girl you don't really want to date anymore, so that you can appear to be attractive to other women. I want an equal playing ground. I am not going to sit here and wait around for you to grow a pair of balls. And, I don't want to hear "I haven't talked to her about breaking up again because I don't want to hurt her feelings" excuses. What about my feelings? See ladies… it's not about him liking you, it's about you liking him. Otherwise, he is just another coward walking the streets blaming everyone else for his lack of, well, whatever.

So… don't tell me how great I am and that you can't believe that no one has just scooped me up and showered me with attention. Don't tell me that I am intriguing and amazing… unless you are going to do something about it. Oh, yeah… you can't… because you have a girlfriend. Next, she'll be pregnant. And… don't hide behind the crap about hurting other people's feelings or being a single dad, or being bad at dating. I've heard them all, and it's still crap.

Be accountable for your own issues and don't bring me into your unfinished business.

...the JUST SEX MAN

I f it's just sex, it's going to have an expiration date, and a disclaimer that says *"this will hurt when you admit to yourself what you are doing"*.

There is no such thing as *"just sex"* for a woman.

It always means something...because we are built that way. We talk, we emote, we ruminate, we analyze, we think and rethink and rethink.

Why?

Because we attach.

It's normal, so don't convince yourself that "if he can do it, you can do it". If you do that, you will be minimizing your worth and hence, your self esteem. Next you'll be saying, "Something is better than nothing". Meanwhile... you are missing out, on, well, something else.

When all is said and done, it is what it is. If a guy says he doesn't want to be in a relationship... he doesn't want to be in a relationship. Period. Having sex with him will not change that. Great sex won't change that.

So buy a toy and some batteries.

...the JACK HAMMER MAN

B ADADADADA!
BADADADADA!
Know what I mean? Does he know there's a person under there?

It's sad, but these are the times I would wish for the 4 MINUTE MAN... right?

Well, he's probably watched too much porn and is trying too hard. What do you do? Hell, I don't know...get him to stop. Kidding. It's best to talk about these things so that you can see if you are capable of being sexually compatible. It doesn't always come naturally... no pun intended.

Ask him what he likes... so that he will ask you what you like. Then you can say, *"Quit pounding me!"*

Sorry, I know it's not funny. You could say whatever you want. And if he asks how he is doing, try to be gentle, but honest. If he is offended, he'll get over it... if he wants to have sex again.

If he persists.... there's your answer.

You need a different partner.

SOME MORE THINGS THAT I KNOW

If it looks like a duck and walks like a duck and talks like a duck... it's probably a duck. That's from AA. In other words, don't try to make excuses for what you see is already there. Inexcusable behavior is and will always be defined as, inexcusable behavior.

A lot of change and empowerment is about shifting your perceptions. When you think in a healthy manner, you attract healthier stuff. So, get out of that fearful thought barrier.

Learn to 'not take the bait'. Taking someone else's bait means that they don't have to take responsibility or be accountable. In other words, you will get hooked into their issues and more than likely start taking emotional responsibility for them. That's why people stay in abusive relationships. They end up thinking it was their fault or that they caused the abuse in some way.

Men come full circle, just watch and trust. If you don't allow things to bother you so much, they come back. There is empowerment in making your own decisions, living your own life and filling your own time.

We learn through relationship and fellowship. This goes back to the concept that relationships are reflections and that we crave the sense of belonging. When we are reflecting our issues through a relationship with another person, we do feel as if we belong there. It is unfortunate that sometimes, as we grow, we feel the need to move on, especially if our partner chooses not to grow.

Pets are much easier than men. They just are.

High maintenance means high quality (in women). There is nothing wrong with knowing what you want. There is nothing wrong with having good boundaries. There is nothing wrong with speaking your truth. Just don't use these concepts to control others.

Vulnerability symbolizes loss of freedom to men. I could write a book on why people feel that doing the right thing or courting a potential partner could feel like it creates an obligation. Making a person feel dispensable only keeps them around if they are unhealthy.

Behaviors should match feelings. Confusion only gives a sense of power to the person creating it... and it's false and doesn't really exist. Let them hallucinate and just walk away. It doesn't matter that they don't understand.

You can't walk away from unconditional love. People don't realize that they want it, or need it, and I wonder if half of us even awaken to the fact that it's there. It just feels good and our souls know it's correct...so we are drawn to it.

You choose your own level of personal growth. It's just like when you exercise, or don't exercise. It's your butt. You either stay unhealthy, or the desire to change overcomes your fear of staying where you are.

Don't sabotage yourself with hopefulness about the wrong things. It is what it is. You cannot, will not, should not, try to change another human being. If you set boundaries, that is enough. If they don't get it, more than likely, they don't know that they don't know. In that case, they aren't going to change anyway. It's unfortunate, but timing is everything.

If the relationship doesn't add value to your life, get rid of it. Ask yourself honestly. Don't make things up to give yourself permission to stay.

Check your motives and what you really want. Are you just scared of being alone? Are you concerned about your time clock? Are you competing with your friends? Don't allow those things to keep you from finding the guy who is really right for you. If you are dishonest with your own motives, that is what you will attract for yourself.

You can't make logic of an illogical situation. Go back to the paragraph about the duck.

It's about you wanting him, not him wanting you. You are giving the test and he is taking it. Don't give him all the answers. Just give the answers that pertain to you.

Women should be nicer to each other. Keep your enemies close. Just kidding, other women are not my enemies. If we do not stick together as women, how are we supposed to build the support to make changes? That's probably how we got into this mess, by promoting a lack of awareness. I think that one of the reasons that men are the way they are is because we train them by settling ourselves. We are so scared of being alone and what others will think of us if we are alone, that we settle. Better to have something instead of nothing. Well, that's a crock. We need to stop competing with each other and focus on ourselves... like men do.

The only person you have to compete with is you.

Once you are aware of what your issues are, it's your responsibility to fix them. Denial ain't just a river in Egypt. Get a grip, get over yourself and get on with your personal growth. You can't break cycles if you remain in them.

Sometimes, he's not the guy you want, he's the guy you have, and that does not mean that you have to stay with him for an inordinate amount of time. Pay attention to the value quotient.

Don't "turn into" the guy you are dating. Keep your identity. It's probably why he liked you in the first place. You don't have to like everything, do everything, feel everything and wear everything that he likes. That really bugs me. Why even work on your own identity if you are just going to adopt someone else's. Think about how weird that is for your friends. Unless you are one of those people that have no time for friends when you are dating somebody. See... there are women who need warning labels too!

Be careful not to attach the wrong meaning to the right thing, or the right meaning to the wrong thing.

Don't wait until there are enough red flags flailing for a half time show, to step aside.

There is no substitute for time, when getting to know someone...so take it.

And last, but not least...

There is nothing wrong with my butt... just so you know. But thanks for the material... I think I've finally gotten enough mileage out of it.

IN CLOSING....

So, there you have it. I guess I am yet another real-life Carrie Bradshaw with a little Samantha Jones thrown in. They're popping up all over the place. One of my very best friends asked me "So, who is your perfect man?". Well, I always say that my car is the perfect man. It goes fast when I want it to, and slow when I need it. It's pretty and makes that really cool car sound. It doesn't talk back or complain and has been reliable over time. It's there every morning and I can't wait to see it. But, I know I can always get a new one. Attach a lawn mower blade to it and that would be the icing on the cake! (Or fertilizer on the lawn)! Otherwise, I guess it's back to 'batteries not included, some assembly required'. Sorry, mom.

On a more serious note, keep in mind that I realize that many of the descriptions of the "men" in this literary extravaganza run together. I wanted to present some thoughts, ideas, experience, strength, and hope, in a humorous tone. I also wanted all who read this through to try to make it a goal for themselves, to recognize their own patterns of behavior. Relationships really are reflections and recognizing those reflections or patterns can be very empowering, especially when change is involved. Positive change builds confidence and that confidence can help us to think twice before we repeat what is just simply comfortable, familiar, and usually pretty unhealthy.

I also want to bring forth this thought, that if this book made you think about just one thing or laugh or relate in any way, then my job is done. I was not looking to write a textbook and I know that this is not the most substantial of therapy books. But...there is therapeutic content here...it's just a little hidden. I did disclose some of my experiences and those of people around me. I am human, I make mistakes and I do stupid stuff sometimes. I just don't do it for a long time anymore.

But occasionally, I have to go back and try it again, just to make sure it still hurts. It does. So, if you can suspend judgment, I'd appreciate it.

Oh, and only the names have been changed to protect the guilty. You all know who you are anyway.

Here are 3 rules we, as women, should follow at all times:

1. **Never** have sex when you don't want to have sex, or before you are ready. It's **unhealthy**.

2. **Never, ever** use sex as a weapon. It's rude and **ineffective.**

3. **Never, ever, ever** get pregnant on purpose, thinking it will make him come back, or love you, or stay, or marry you, or keep him from cheating. It's just plain **wrong** and affects too many people including the one on the way.

You get what you deserve, but you determine what you deserve.

Remember girls, don't act powerless because you want him... be and act empowered so that he'll want you. High maintenance means high quality. And, for the record, marriage isn't necessarily the prize. It is much more than that and shouldn't be dealt with like a game you are trying to win. You can always win. But, it is not a win/lose situation. If he thinks of marriage as, just a piece of paper, then to him, that is all that it is, a piece of paper. Look at the reality of the situation. There is dating material, and there is relationship material. In reality, marriage is only the beginning of a true relationship, based on unconditional love, respect and trust. It's up to you what the ending will be, and that's the prize... or surprise, depending on how you deal with it.

In all honesty, though, no one is perfect, especially, not me. We pick emotionally unavailable men because we've gotten inconsistent reinforcement in our lives. It may have been from our parents, since we act out what we learn in our families. It may have been from other authority figures, siblings, or peers. In any case, the unpredictability of inconsistent reinforcement can make one feel as if, he or she, is not good enough. So, we put up with crap we shouldn't and constantly try to prove ourselves. Or... we just give up and take what we can get. Or.... we try to fix ourselves, by fixing "it". Remember... you can only control yourself... not him and not the outcome.

Awareness empowers you. Empowerment helps your self-esteem. Healthy self-esteem helps you to make healthy decisions. Those decisions can make your life so much more productive, and exhilarating. You will be more motivated, yet content and at peace. Don't you want peace? I want all of those things. So, break a few cycles and make yourself an example for other women, and well, men too.

And for the last time....

SOMEBODY, PLEASE!! CUT MY GRASS!!

EPILOG

Thanks, I feel much better, and I hope you enjoyed reading this as much as I enjoyed writing it. Stay tuned. There's more on the way (because I couldn't fit it all in one book), only next time, it's about fixing my roof or building a deck. We'll see.

This has been a cathartic experience for me, obviously. It helped me to truly focus on what I want, as opposed to what I don't want. It's hard to stick with that focus sometimes, because it means that you have to believe that there is another way. Thinking about what you want is much more positive and conducive for a life of health and contentment.

So, I have news that in the process of this book coming to fruition, there he appeared. I had my random moment and met the "man in my head". He did all the right things. He courted me and took me on dates that he planned. He brought me flowers and made it clear that he wanted to be with me. I didn't have to wonder or question what his motives were. He is as close to "TPM" (The Perfect Man) as I could want. He has some of the characteristics of many of the men in this book, of course. But, they are just characteristics. We work things out as they come and I trust that he will be there to work those things out. All in all, he is just awesome. I am very fortunate.

To him I say thank you for being supportive of this process and of our process. It takes a mature man to be emotionally available and supportive while his significant other publishes a book about men. But most importantly... thank you FOR CUTTING MY GRASS!! (Which he did on our first all day date, without me asking.)

Thank you also to all of my wonderful girlfriends for all the material and support over all the years... and thanks Mom for the advice. You were pretty right about pretty much everything. I guess that's why you are still married to Dad.

Sonia

P.S.

If you want crappy things to stop happening to you, stop accepting them, stop participating in them and demand more.

www.ingramcontent.com/pod-product-compliance
Lightning Source LLC
Chambersburg PA
CBHW030024290326
41934CB00005B/477